Fixing Our Eyes on Jesus

Fixing Our Eyes on Jesus

Devotional Encouragement for Weary Pastors

ADAM WYATT

Foreword by Dean Inserra

RESOURCE *Publications* · Eugene, Oregon

FIXING OUR EYES ON JESUS
Devotional Encouragement for Weary Pastors

Copyright © 2024 Adam Wyatt. All rights reserved. Except for brief quotations in critical publications or reviews, no part of this book may be reproduced in any manner without prior written permission from the publisher. Write: Permissions, Wipf and Stock Publishers, 199 W. 8th Ave., Suite 3, Eugene, OR 97401.

Resource Publications
An Imprint of Wipf and Stock Publishers
199 W. 8th Ave., Suite 3
Eugene, OR 97401

www.wipfandstock.com

PAPERBACK ISBN: 979-8-3852-1315-3
HARDCOVER ISBN: 979-8-3852-1316-0
EBOOK ISBN: 979-8-3852-1317-7

04/24/24

Scripture quotations taken from the (NASB®) New American Standard Bible®, Copyright © 1960, 1971, 1977, 1995, 2020 by The Lockman Foundation. Used by permission. All rights reserved. lockman.org

CONTENTS

Foreword by Dean Inserra | vii
Day 1: Jesus helps us by giving us a greater vision of God's glory | 1
Day 2: Jesus helps us by reminding us of the power of His word | 3
Day 3: Jesus helps us by reminding us of His unchanging nature and faithfulness. | 6
Day 4: Jesus helps us by identifying with our personal struggles and weaknesses. | 8
Day 5: Jesus helps us by giving us hope for the future. | 10
Day 6: Jesus helps us by reminding us that we share in a heavenly calling. | 12
Day 7: Jesus helps us by reminding us to fix our thoughts on Him and His faithfulness | 14
Day 8: Jesus helps us by reminding us of the importance of perseverance and obedience. | 16
Day 9: Jesus helps us by giving us rest when we are weary. | 18
Day 10: Jesus helps us by providing us with mercy and grace as our great high priest in our time of need. | 20
Day 11: Jesus helps us by reminding us to rely on God the Father for strength. | 22
Day 12: Jesus helps us by being our perfect example of obedience to God. | 24

CONTENTS

Day 13: Jesus helps us by giving us an eternal hope that does not disappoint. | 26

Day 14: Jesus helps us by being our anchor in times of trouble. | 28

Day 15: Jesus helps us by reminding us of His power to save people. | 30

Day 16: Jesus helps us by offering a better covenant based on better promises. | 32

Day 17: Jesus helps us by reminding us of the power of His forgiveness. | 34

Day 18: Jesus helps us by reminding us to persevere in faith, even when things are hard. | 36

Day 19: Jesus helps us by offering Himself as the sacrifice for our sins once and for all. | 38

Day 20: Jesus helps us by giving us the strength to endure trials and persecution. | 40

Day 21: Jesus helps us by assuring us that we are saved through faith in Him. | 42

Day 22: Jesus helps us by reminding us of the faith and perseverance of those who have gone before us | 44

Day 23: Jesus helps us by reminding us of the power of prayer. | 46

Day 24: Jesus helps us by reminding us of the ultimate reward that awaits us. | 48

Day 25: Jesus helps us by reminding us of the importance of living by faith, not by sight. | 50

Day 26: Jesus helps us by being the author and perfecter of our faith | 52

Day 27: Jesus helps us by being the source of our joy and strength in life. | 54

Day 28: Jesus helps us by disciplining us for our good. | 56

Day 29: Jesus helps us by providing our peace and security. | 58

Day 30: Jesus helps us by empowering us to offer sacrifices of praise and good deeds. | 60

FOREWORD

"Is there a devotional you can recommend?" I get asked the question regularly as a pastor. It encourages me to see church members desiring to have a devotional guide to help take them through the scriptures. Interestingly enough, I have never been asked that question by another pastor for himself. We swap book suggestions regularly, but it has never been about personal devotional suggestion. While we are Christians first before we are pastors, and can benefit from any devotional that is faithful to the scriptures, what if there was a devotional written with us in mind? In an era where it seems to be open season on disparaging and discouraging pastors, perhaps a devotional written with us specifically in mind, is exactly what we need. I am currently more aware of my need to stay close to the Lord, and maintain clean hands and a pure heart, more than any other time in my ministry life. Yes, I have always thought that was important, but I feel a different urgency in our cultural moment.

    Far too many pastors are struggling. We were never promised an easy road in this calling of ours to local church leadership, so this shouldn't be seen as a grievance or a surprise. Being a pastor is certainly not for those who lack resilience. Simultaneously, it is also a great privilege to be given the opportunity to open our bibles and preach to the congregation God has allowed us to shepherd. I do believe there is far more good than bad in pastoral leadership, but the bad seems to magnify itself in our hearts and minds if we are not careful. We need to maintain a steady and consistent devotional life to first stay relationally close to the Lord, but also to remember the glorious calling of pastoral ministry.

I am thankful Pastor Adam Wyatt has stepped into the role of a Barnabas and has chosen to be an encouragement to pastors through a devotional written to his fellow brothers, using the book of Hebrews as the source and guide. A devotional written to and for pastors is something I absolutely need, and I'm guessing you do too, pastor. Please see this as a Christ-focused, scripturally saturated, call to endure for the sake of the gospel mission and our local churches to which we've been entrusted.

Dean Inserra, pastor of City Church, Tallahassee and author of *The Unsaved Christian*.

DAY 1

Jesus helps us by giving us a greater vision of God's glory

"And He is the radiance of His glory and the exact representation of His nature, and upholds all things by the word of His power. When He had made purification of sins, He sat down at the right hand of the Majesty on high, having become so much better than the angels, to the extent that He has inherited a more excellent name than they.."

(HEBREWS 1:3-4)

Pastor,

In times of difficulty and uncertainty, feeling overwhelmed and discouraged is easy. But as we reflect on Hebrews 1:3-4, we can find comfort and encouragement in the fact that Jesus is the radiance of God's glory. This means that when we look to Jesus, we see God's very nature and character on full display. Jesus is the perfect representation of God, and in Him, we see God's holiness, love, and infinite power. Meditating on this truth can remind us of three practical applications to help us in our ministry.

First, Jesus' glory reminds us of God's faithfulness. It can be easy to doubt God's goodness and faithfulness during difficult circumstances. But when we look to Jesus, we see God is always faithful to keep His promises. Jesus fulfilled countless prophecies about the Messiah, demonstrating God's unwavering commitment to His people. So, as we face challenges and trials in our ministry, we can trust that, just as God was faithful to Israel, He will certainly remain faithful to us and the work He has called us to do.

Second, Jesus' glory reminds us of God's power. When we feel weak and inadequate for the task, we can take heart in the fact that Jesus is the radiance of God's glory. In Him, we see the power of God on full display. Jesus healed the sick, raised the dead, and calmed the storm, and, in so doing, He demonstrated that nothing is impossible for God. So pastor, as we face difficult circumstances in our ministry, we can draw on God's power to overcome any and all obstacles and accomplish His purposes in the ministry that He has called us to.

Let us be encouraged by the fact that Jesus is the radiance of God's glory. As we reflect on this truth, may we be reminded of God's faithfulness, power, and His great love. And may we take heart in the knowledge that we serve a God worthy of all praise and glory. So, stay the course and trust in Him, for He is faithful and He is faithful to us.

Questions for Reflection:

1. How has God been faithful to you and your ministry in the past?

2. If God has been faithful to you and your ministry in the past, what makes you think He won't continue doing that?

3. How can you see the glory of Christ in your life today? List them.

DAY 2

Jesus helps us by reminding us of the power of His word (Hebrews 1:1–3)

"God, after He spoke long ago to the fathers in the prophets in many portions and in many ways, in these last days has spoken to us in *His* Son, whom He appointed heir of all things, through whom He also made the world. And He is the radiance of His glory and the exact representation of His nature, and [e]upholds all things by the word of His power."

(HEBREWS 1:1–3)

Pastor,

As we continue to labor in the ministry of the word, we can sometimes forget the power of what He has already clearly said in His word. In times of difficulty and uncertainty, it's sometimes easy to feel lost and unsure how to proceed because we can question where we might be headed. But as we reflect on Hebrews 1:1–3, we can find comfort and guidance in the fact that God has spoken in His word and continues to do so today.

We often remind our church members of the power of God's word in their lives. Still, *we* also must also be reminded that the Bible is not just a collection of stories and moral teachings but a living and active communication from God Himself. He has spoken, and He will continue speaking and He will speak to us. So, as we meditate on this truth, we can be reminded of three practical applications that can help us in our ministry.

First, God's word reminds us of His sovereignty. Amid difficult circumstances, it can be easy to feel like everything is out of control. But when we read the Bible, time and time again, we see that God is in charge of all things. He created the world, sustains it, and has a plan for it and He has a plan for you and your ministry. As we face challenges in our ministry, we can trust that God is still in control and His plan will ultimately prevail, even in our ministries.

Second, God's word reminds us of His infinite wisdom. When we feel unsure of how to proceed, we can take comfort in knowing that God speaks through His word. Clearly. The Bible truly is a source of spiritual wisdom and guidance, ready and waiting to aid us in every challenge we face. As pastors navigating difficult circumstances, we can rest assured that the Holy Scriptures contain the necessary direction to lead our congregations through the storms of life. But we must also remember that God's Word must speak to *us*. So let us look to the Word of God, and allow its unerring and perfect counsel guide us toward the good path for our ministry.

Third, God's word reminds us of His glorious grace. When we feel overwhelmed by our own failures and shortcomings, which are many, we can take heart in the fact that God speaks and speaks clearly of His grace through His word. In the Bible, we find the story of God's redemptive plan for humanity and His personal redemptive plan for our souls. As we minister to others, we can offer them the same message of hope and grace that we also find in the Bible.

Dear pastor, let us be encouraged by the fact that God speaks through His word. He does not just speak to our churches; He speaks to us. As we reflect on this truth, may we be reminded of His sovereignty, wisdom, and grace. And may we take heart in the knowledge that we serve a God who is always speaking and guiding us through His word.

DAY 2

Questions for Reflection:

1. How do you need to be reminded that God still speaks to us?

2. What is God teaching you through His word during this season of your ministry and life?

3. How do you see God's daily grace in your life? Have you thanked Him for them?

DAY 3

Jesus helps us by reminding us of His unchanging nature and faithfulness.

"You, Lord, in the beginning laid the foundation of the earth, and the heavens are the works of Your hands; They will perish, but You remain; And they all will wear out like a garment, nd like a robe you will roll them up; like a garment they will also be changed. But you are the same, And your years will not come to an end."
(HEBREWS 1:10–12)

Pastor,

As we navigate through life's difficult circumstances, even in our ministry, we can take comfort in the unchanging nature of our God. In Hebrews 1:10–12, we read that God does not change, even as the heavens and earth may pass away. This truth is a rock-solid foundation upon which we can anchor our faith and hope in a world that is constantly changing.

God does not change. Remember that. Savor that. The God that called you into ministry is the same God leading through whatever situation you find yourself in. He is good. He is gracious. He is kind. He laid the foundation of the earth in the beginning, and his years have no end. His will always come to pass. Trust Him.

In times of uncertainty, difficulty, and turmoil, looking to other sources for comfort and stability can often be tempting. But our comfort cannot come from our church budget or attendance

DAY 3

or applause of men. It cannot come from our preaching. It cannot come from our effort. Everything in our ministry can change, for good or for evil. But remember that our God is unchanging; His goodness and character are constant. He is the same yesterday, today, and forever, and we can trust Him to be faithful in all things.

As pastors, we are called to lead and guide our congregations through challenging times. But we can take heart in the knowledge that our God is with us and will not forsake us. We find a firm foundation to build our ministry upon, and we find hope in His unchanging nature.

As we meditate on God's unchanging nature, we can be reminded of His sovereignty and trustworthiness. He is the Almighty One who holds all things in His hands. He is the only One who we can trust to work all things together for good for those of us who love Him. He is the God who is faithful to keep all of His promises and He always keeps His word.

Pastor, be encouraged by the unchanging nature of our good God. Whatever we face, let us trust in His sovereignty and faithfulness. Let us anchor our hope in the unchanging character of our Lord and Savior, Jesus Christ, who is the same yesterday, today, and forever and is the same one who loves our church and wants the best for her. May we, as pastors, love and lead our churches in the confidence that we have that our God does not change.

Questions for Reflection:

1. What is one thing you wish you could change about your current situation?

2. How can knowing that God is the same today as He was yesterday help you find peace whether what you wish could be different actually changes?

3. How has God continued to be "steady" in your life lately?

DAY 4

Jesus helps us by identifying with our personal struggles and weaknesses.

"Therefore, in all things He had to be made like His brothers so that He might become a merciful and faithful high priest in things pertaining to God, to make propitiation for the sins of the people. For since He Himself was tempted in that which He has suffered, He is able to come to the aid of those who are tempted."

(HEBREWS 2:17–18)

Pastor,

No matter what people think about us, we struggle and are weak. We are sinful and we are frail. Honestly, we have to come to terms with the fact the ministries we have been called to are too much for us to succeed apart from God's power in our lives.

We have sinned. We have weaknesses and are not immune to struggles. Jesus understands. He was made like us in every way, yet He never sinned. Because of this, He can understand and sympathize with us in our weaknesses, whatever they are.

But, despite these struggles and weaknesses, we have been called to faithfully serve and shepherd our people. Yet, the struggles we face and endure can often leave us feeling discouraged, broken, or lonely and unequipped to serve them. But, in Jesus Christ, we have a perfect example of how to live in our weaknesses.

DAY 4

Jesus faced temptation and endured suffering and even death. Yet He remained faithful to His calling and perfectly obedient to His Father, showing us that even in our many weakness, we can still trust in God's strength and power to carry us through.

We can learn from this text that it is ok to ask for help. In fact, we need to ask for help. Through prayer, Jesus sought support for His ministry from God the Father and used His disciples to help Him fulfill it. Pastor, you also need to pray and ask others for help. There is no shame in this. Rather, we need to follow the example of Christ by doing it.

Another thing that we must learn is that it is ok to be vulnerable. Just asking for help reminds us that we do not all have it figured out. This is a good thing because it reminds us to look to the One who understands us and can give us the help we truly need. Be vulnerable. Look to Jesus.

Pastor, let us take comfort in the example of Jesus. He is our perfect example of how to live despite our human and ministry weaknesses. May we lean into His strength and trust in His power to carry us through our weakness.

Questions for Reflection:

1. How can understanding our weaknesses actually help us in ministry?

2. How have you sought God in your personal weaknesses?

3. What must you personally repent of to be more used by God?

DAY 5

Jesus helps us by giving us hope for the future.

"For in subjecting all things to him, He left nothing that is not subject to him. But now we do not yet see all things subjected to him."
(HEBREWS 2:8)

Pastor,

Have you ever stopped to contemplate what is outside of your control? Honestly, everything. There is not one thing that is in your control. Sure, you have choices to make and things to do, but God and God alone is the One and the only one in control of all things.

This should actually bring us comfort. This should bring us peace. While you may be suffering in the present and going through incredible difficulties, God is in total control. You may be dealing with untold challenges, but God is subjecting everything to Himself, so take heart.

Charles Spurgeon once said, "Remember this, had any other condition been better for you than the one in which you are, divine love would have put you there." And, as he usually is, Spurgeon is correct in this assessment. God knows you and your ministry, and he has placed you uniquely in your situation, regardless of what it looks like. And, remember, He is still in absolute control of all things and He will sustain you.

Because God is in control, we can face circumstances by trusting Him. This gives us hope for the future, no matter what the present looks like. Instead of being overwhelmed by your current

DAY 5

situation, trust the sovereignty of God in all things and trust Him to see you through whatever you are going through.

Additionally, because we know God is in control, we can boldly approach Him for help through prayer. Only because we know God is in control of everything can we hope to see prayer be effective. So, trust Him to continue to be good to you in the present as you expectantly trust Him with your future.

Pastor, be bold. Be strong. Be faithful. For God is in control of all things.

Questions for Reflection:

1. How have you seen God be good to you and your ministry in the past?

2. What specifically in your ministry do you need to trust God with?

3. What is keeping you from trusting God fully today?

DAY 6

Jesus helps us by reminding us that we share in a heavenly calling.

"Therefore, holy brothers *and sisters*, partakers of a heavenly calling, consider the Apostle and High Priest of our confession: Jesus; He was faithful to Him who appointed Him, as Moses also was in all His house."
(HEBREWS 3:1–2)

Pastor,

When was the last time you stopped to consider our glorious calling to serve Christ? Seriously? When was the last time you stopped and counted yourself honored to serve the Lord in ministry? It is a heavenly calling, to be sure, even when it is difficult.

It can sometimes be easy to lose sight of the purpose and honor behind your calling. We often wonder if our efforts are making any difference. We wonder if anyone is really listening to the messages we preach week after week. We wonder if anyone understands the weight that we carry. We wonder if we are making any difference in the people we both love and serve. But in this passage, we are reminded that we share a heavenly calling that is much bigger than ourselves. The calling is heavy at times, but it is also heavenly. We have been called to lead others in their faith and to guide them toward a deeper understanding of God's truth. Is there anything more noble than this?

It's easy to get caught up in the day-to-day tasks of pastoral ministry. Still, it's important to remember that we ultimately serve

DAY 6

the Lord as we serve others. When we fix our thoughts on Jesus Christ, we can find the strength to persevere through difficult times. No matter what they are. Like Moses, Jesus was faithful to the one who appointed Him. We, too, can trust that God will give us the strength and wisdom to fulfill our heavenly calling because He is the One who has also called us to it.

Pastor, if you're feeling discouraged or overwhelmed in your current ministry or situation, take heart in the knowledge that you are part of a far greater purpose. Fix your thoughts on our glorious Christ, the author and perfecter of our faith and of our ministry, and let His perfect faithful example inspire you to keep pressing forward in faithfulness. Remember that you are not alone in your struggles. Remember that God will give you the strength to carry out His calling in your life. Stay the course.

Questions for Reflection:

1. How does looking at our ministry problems keep us from remembering that we have a heavenly calling?

2. What do you need to do to stay faithful to this heavenly calling?

3. How does this heavenly calling humble you?

DAY 7

Jesus helps us by reminding us to fix our thoughts on Him and His faithfulness

"Therefore, holy brothers *and sisters*, partakers of a heavenly calling, consider the Apostle and High Priest of our confession: Jesus; He was faithful to Him who appointed Him, as Moses also was in all His house."
(HEBREWS 3:1–2)

Pastor,

The desire to be faithful in ministry is often at the forefront of our minds. But as we navigate the challenges and difficulties of pastoral work, it can be easy to lose sight of what it truly means to be faithful because we can often lose sight of it by trying to be successful. So, in your current context, do you genuinely desire to be *faithful* in ministry?

In Hebrews 3:1-2, we are reminded that Jesus is our ultimate example of faithfulness. As it says, Jesus was "faithful to him who appointed him." God has appointed us. So, in order to be faithful in ministry, we must focus on Jesus and His example of unwavering faithfulness in faithfully carrying out the work God has called us to do. This means persevering through trials, showing love and compassion to those we minister to, and always seeking to grow in our relationship with God.

But even as we seek to be faithful, we must remember that our strength is incredibly self-limited. We *will* face moments of weariness and discouragement, and we *will* sometimes feel like we are not making a difference to those to whom we minister. However, in these moments, we must turn to Jesus and rely on His strength to carry us through.

So, dear pastor, if you desire to be faithful in ministry, remember that it must be a genuine desire that God has placed in your heart. Fix your eyes on Jesus, and let His example of faithfulness inspire you to keep pressing forward. And when you feel the weariest and most heavy-hearted, lean into His strength and trust that He will carry you through.

Questions for Reflection:

1. What unhealthy thoughts consume your mind rather than the supremacy of Jesus?

2. How does it comfort you to know that Jesus has appointed you to your present task of ministry?

3. How is it freeing to know that in your weaknesses, Christ wants to see you through?

DAY 8

Jesus helps us by reminding us of the importance of perseverance and obedience.

"Take care, brothers *and sisters*, that there will not be in any one of you an evil, unbelieving heart that falls away from the living God.

(HEBREWS 3:12)

Pastor,

Ministry is a glorious and heavenly calling. But it is difficult. No one but a fellow pastor could genuinely understand the incredible difficulty of the calling placed upon you. It is hard, and often, makes many tap out and quit under its burden.

But Hebrews 3:12 reminds us of the importance of remaining faithful. As pastors, we are called to remain steadfast in our work and not give up, even when we face trials and difficulties. It warns us of the great danger of tapping out, of giving in to the temptation to turn away from God and His calling on our lives.

The text also says, "Take care, brothers, lest there be in any of you an evil, unbelieving heart, leading you to fall away from the living God." In other words, we must guard our hearts lest we become disillusioned and lose sight of God's glorious purpose for our lives and of our ministry. We focus much on staying the course in our ministry, but we must also be reminded that our ability to stay the course is dependent upon standing firm in our faith!

But how can we remain faithful in the face of discouragement and weariness? The key is that we must fix our eyes on Jesus, just as

DAY 8

Hebrews 12:2 tells us. He is the ultimate example of perseverance and faithfulness, and He can and will give us the strength to keep pressing on despite our difficulties and challenges.

We can also find encouragement and support in our fellow brothers and Christ. Especially those who are in the ministry. As Hebrews 3:13 says, "But exhort one another every day, as long as it is called 'today,' that none of you may be hardened by the deceitfulness of sin." By surrounding ourselves with other believers and brothers and sisters in ministry who can lift us up and hold us accountable, we can stay strong in our faith and resist the temptation to give up.

Pastor, remember the importance of remaining faithful if you are feeling weary and discouraged in your pastoral work. Fix your eyes on Jesus Christ, seek encouragement from your fellow brothers, and trust that God will give you the strength you need to keep pressing forward.

Questions for Reflection:

1. How can you guard against a sinful, unbelieving heart that could lead you to turn away from God and the ministry?

2. What practical steps can you take to nurture faithfulness in your ministry and faith?

3. How can you encourage another pastor who may be dealing with discouragement?

DAY 9

Jesus helps us by giving us rest when we are weary.

"Consequently, there remains a Sabbath rest for the people of God. For the one who has entered His rest has himself also rested from his works, as God did from His."

(HEBREWS 4:9–10)

Pastor,

Ministry can be exhausting, and it can be all too easy to get caught up in the constant demands and pressures of serving others. It is truly noble work but can wear us down, even in the best of seasons. So, when we are tired, wearied, or stressed, we must look to Christ for our rest.

As pastors, we must remember that we are not called to rely on our strength and abilities while we serve but to lean wholly on Christ, who promises us rest and renewal. Hebrews 4:9–10 reminds us of this important truth. This rest is not merely physical, although that is important, but a spiritual rest that comes from our trust in the finished work of Christ. As we turn to Him in faith and surrender, we can find proper rest for our weary and worried souls.

When we are weary and worried, trying to push through in our own strength can be tempting but it is exhausting. Instead, we must intentionally carve out time to rest in God's presence in His word, seek His face, and be still before Him. This may mean setting aside specific times each day for prayer and meditation on

Scripture or taking a more extended Sabbath rest each week to recharge and renew our minds and hearts. Sometimes, it is as simple as taking a nap.

But as we rest in Christ, we can also be reminded that our work is not in vain. While we may sometimes feel weary and discouraged, we can trust that God is using our efforts for His purposes and glory. Our job is to remain faithful and obedient, even when amidst great difficulties, knowing that our reward is ultimately in Christ.

So, fellow pastor, let us take heart and find our true Sabbath rest in Christ, trusting that He will sustain us through every season of our ministry. Let us surrender our burdens and cares to Him, and allow Him to refresh and renew us so that we may continue to serve Him with joy and passion, even in weariness and stress.

Questions for Reflection:

1. How have you responded to seasons of weariness in your ministry in the past?

2. What are some ways that you can prioritize rest in your current season of ministry?

3. How does the promised reward of eternal rest challenge you to remain faithful today?

DAY 10

Jesus helps us by providing us with mercy and grace as our great high priest in our time of need.

"Therefore, since we have a great high priest who has passed through the heavens, Jesus the Son of God, let's hold firmly to our confession. For we do not have a high priest who cannot sympathize with our weaknesses, but One who has been tempted in all things just as *we are, yet* without sin. Therefore let's approach the throne of grace with confidence, so that we may receive mercy and find grace for help at the time of *our* need."

(HEBREWS 4:14–16)

Pastor,

Isn't it a glorious reminder that Jesus provides us mercy and grace? Hebrews 4:14–16 reminds us that we have a great and glorious high priest who can sympathize with our weaknesses and offer us the help we need in our lives and ministry. When we face trials and difficulties in ministry, it can be easy to feel discouraged and overwhelmed. Jesus, as our great high priest, understands these personal struggles and temptations because he has experienced them. Yet, he did not sin. And, as our sinless high priest, Jesus offers us mercy and grace to help us in our times of dearest need.

Because we know that we have a high priest who understands our struggles and offers us grace and mercy, we can approach him confidently, knowing that he will not turn us away but will welcome us with open arms. We have an incredible privilege as ministers of His Gospel to come to God boldly and confidently because of what Jesus has done for us. May we never take this for granted, but rather, may we draw near to God daily, seeking His mercy and grace to help us in our trials and ministry struggles.

Let us, therefore, come boldly to the throne of grace, that we may obtain mercy and find grace to help in time of need and may we trust in the mercy and grace of our great high priest and find the strength and courage we need to continue faithfully in our ministries.

Questions for Reflection:

1. How does knowing that Jesus is our High Priest encourage you to come boldly before the throne of grace?

2. In what ways do you tend to rely on your own works rather than relying on Jesus as your High Priest?

3. How can you encourage those around you to come boldly to Jesus?

DAY 11

Jesus helps us by reminding us to rely on God the Father for strength.

"In the days of His humanity, He offered up both prayers and pleas with loud crying and tears to the One able to save Him from death, and He was heard because of His devout behavior"

(HEBREWS 5:7)

Pastor,

When was the last time you realized that apart from trusting in the Lord, you are not truly–in your own strength–capable of thriving in the ministry that God has called you? Indeed, pastors can get to some sort of level of 'success' if they are faithful to preach and love people, but there will come a time in pastoral ministry when you will be reminded that the things you are going through are totally out of your control and without the move of God in your life, you are without hope.

In these times, it is important to learn to treasure these moments. These moments give you time to seek the Lord in ways your confidence may not truly allow. Hebrews 5:7 tells us that Jesus Himself, the sovereign Lord of the entire cosmos, cried out with loud cries and tears to His heavenly Father. Scripture tells us that He prayed with sweat drops of blood. But Scripture also teaches us that He was totally consumed with His Father's will.

In this way, Jesus is a beautiful example of not trusting in Himself for His own strength. If the sovereign Lord of the universe prayed for strength, how can you, frail man, do the life-giving work of pastoral ministry in your own power? Being reminded of our inadequacies is glorious if it leads us to the trustworthy source of our strength. Being reminded of our weaknesses is glorious if it leads us to the fountain of living waters who can give us strength.

As we consider the psalmist's words in Psalm 46:1, "God is our refuge and strength, a very present help in trouble," let us be reminded that our God is indeed a faithful and true refuge for those of us who genuinely trust in him. When we are weary and burdened and when the trials of ministry seem too great to bear we can turn to Him and find comfort and strength in His arms.

Therefore, I exhort you, my dear brother, to turn to the Lord in your times of trouble and affliction. Do not be afraid to cry out to Him for help, for He truly is our very present help in time of need. Trust in Him, and He *will* sustain you. Lean not on your own understanding, but in all your ways acknowledge him, and he will make your paths straight.

Let us give thanks to our Lord and Savior Jesus Christ, who has borne our griefs and carried our great sorrows, all the way to Calvary, and let us all take heart in His merciful promise to be with us always, even to the end of the age.

Questions for Reflection:

1. What keeps you from trusting the Father in your life?

2. What keeps you from trusting the Father in your family?

3. What keeps you from trusting the Father in your ministry?

DAY 12

Jesus helps us by being our perfect example of obedience to God.

"Although He was a Son, He learned obedience from the things which He suffered. And having been perfected, He became the source of eternal salvation for all those who obey Him."
(HEBREWS 5:8–9)

Pastor,

Are you being obedient in your life and ministry? Most pastors do not have people that ask that question. Most of the time, we are out front in leadership and in preaching, which generally requires that we at least appear like the folks with their spiritual act together. But do we?

When tasked with serving a local church, we tend to urge people towards their obedience. This is right and good. However, who is challenging us towards the same pursuit of obedience?

Being a pastor is not an easy task, and we all realize that it comes with unique challenges. It can be far too easy to get caught up in the struggles of our life or ministry and forget the importance of being obedient to God. But I want to remind you that Jesus helps us by being our perfect example of obedience to God.

Hebrews 5:8–9 reminds us that Jesus, as the Son of God, suffered and learned obedience through His own intense suffering. He endured the cross, despising its shame, so we could have eternal salvation through him. So, we, too, ought to learn obedience as we deal with the struggles of pastoral ministry as we seek to lead others toward salvation and faithfulness. We are not immune from struggles, but we have an excellent opportunity to be molded by them as we learn obedience.

If you struggle with obedience, I want to encourage you to turn to Jesus. Look to His example and allow Him to guide you and your attempt to be faithful amidst your struggle. Spend time in prayer and the Word of God, seeking His wisdom and strength as you attempt to model His obedience. Remember that you are not alone and that Jesus is with you, helping you through every trial and struggle.

So today, dear friend, I pray that you will be filled with a renewed sense of obedience to God, strengthened by Jesus' perfect example, and may you find the courage and wisdom to live a life that is obedient to God's will and you seek to fulfill the ministry that He has called you to. May you be encouraged to press on, knowing that Jesus is with you every step of the way and He is worth it.

Questions for Reflection:

1. What lessons can we learn for our own lives by looking at the perfect obedience of Jesus Christ?

2. How do we tend to focus more on our church members' obedience than our own?

3. How can a renewed obedience to Jesus help us stay faithful in the ministry?

DAY 13

Jesus helps us by giving us an eternal hope that does not disappoint.

"This hope we have as an anchor of the soul, a *hope* both sure and reliable and one which enters within the veil, where Jesus has entered as a forerunner for us, having become a high priest forever according to the order of Melchizedek."

(HEBREWS 6:19–20)

Pastor,

Our lives are but a breath. This means that our ministries are as well. As pastors, we often overestimate what we can do in the short term and underestimate what we can do in the long term. This means we sometimes overlook our ministries in light of eternity.

We have an eternal hope through Christ, knowing that we will one day live in eternity with Him. This should also bring us much comfort in our lives, but it should also bring us much joy as we do the work of the pastor.

We have the fantastic opportunity to do work with eternal significance. This does not mean that we always see it. But, as we place our hope in Christ, we get the opportunity to trust in Him as we do what we do in His name. Is there a better comfort for you?

It can be so easy to get bogged down in the day-to-day tasks of ministry, feeling like we are not making a significant impact.

DAY 13

But that is simply not the case. Every interaction we have, every sermon we preach, and every single act of humble service we perform has the potential to have eternal significance for the people we love and serve. As we place our hope in Christ and trust in His guidance, we can have hope that He is using us for His good purposes, even when we cannot see the results. Trust in Him for those results, knowing that He is the one who brings eternal rewards.

Even when we face challenges or setbacks in our ministries, we can trust that our labor in the Lord is not in vain. For He sees us and He sees what we do. For, we are working for a kingdom that will last forever, and every effort we make in His name has the potential to bear fruit that will last for all eternity.

So as you go about your ministry, remember that your work has eternal significance. Place your hope in Christ, trust in His guidance, and know that your labors of love in the Lord are not in vain. May you find comfort and strength in knowing you are working for a kingdom that will last forever.

And may God bless you and keep you, and may His love and grace sustain you always, for you are working towards eternal rewards in your labor.

Questions for Reflection?

1. How have you seen God bless your service in the past?

2. How can you focus on the eternal fruit that lasts in your service to God?

3. What eternal fruit do you want God to accomplish through you in your current season of ministry? How can you pray for that to happen now?

DAY 14

Jesus helps us by being our anchor in times of trouble.

"This hope we have as an anchor of the soul, a *hope* both sure and reliable and one which enters within the veil, where Jesus has entered as a forerunner for us, having become a high priest forever according to the order of Melchizedek."

(HEBREWS 6:19–20)

Pastor,

Hope is a precious thing. It can bring peace. It can bring healing. It is something that we need daily, especially when we do the sometimes soul-draining work of the gospel ministry. But it can also be elusive if we fail to consider its proper source.

Jesus has gifted us a steadfast anchor for our souls, which will never disappoint, but it is also one that we often treat lightly. As a pastor, you have likely experienced the ups and downs of ministry and life. You have seen the joys of weddings, births, baptisms, and the immense sorrow of funerals and divorce. You have seen people grow in their faith and also those who have made a shipwreck of it.

But through it all, Jesus remains our steadfast anchor in everything. Just as a ship has to rely on an anchor to keep it steady during a storm, we must rely on Jesus to keep us grounded when the storms of life rage. When we face these difficulties in ministry or our lives, we can turn to Jesus and find true and lasting comfort in His unchanging love and faithfulness. Because of His love and

DAY 14

faithfulness, we can trust that He will never leave or forsake us and that He is always working for our good.

Jesus is not just our anchor; He is also our forerunner. He has gone *before* us into the inner sanctuary so we can follow in His footsteps. Through His death and resurrection, Jesus has made a way for us to enter into the very presence of God. But, be reminded, as pastors, we have the privilege of leading others into this *same* hope and assurance.

So, as you go about your ministry, dear pastor, remember that Jesus is your steadfast anchor and the forerunner of your faith. So, when the winds of change or uncertainty blow, and they will, hold fast to Him and trust in His infinite goodness. And as you lead others, point them to the same Anchor, reminding them of the hope that can only be found in Him.

May God bless and keep you, and may His love and grace sustain you always.

Questions for Reflection:

1. What storms are you facing right now?

2. How has your Anchor sustained you in the past?

3. How can you trust Him now, knowing He is good, gracious, and merciful?

DAY 15

Jesus helps us by reminding us of His power to save people.

"Therefore He is also able to save forever those who come to God through Him, since He always lives to make intercession for them."
(Hebrews 7:25)

Pastor,

Jesus came into the world to save people. This is the fundamental basis of our preaching ministry. This reminds us that all we do has the hope of success because we know that God truly wants to save people. Jesus, and Jesus alone, has the power to save to the uttermost those who draw near.

Have you forgotten this in ministry or preaching? Have you gone through a season that seems dry and unfruitful? Have you lost sight of how God wants to save people? Take heart, fellow pastor. For God wants to use you to produce the eternal fruit of salvation. This assures us that our preaching is not in vain!

As pastors, we are privileged to preach and share the Gospel with others and lead them to Christ. But sometimes, we feel like our efforts are not making a difference or that the message of the Gospel is falling on deaf ears. Seasons like this are difficult. But, we can take heart in the truth that God is always at work around and through us.

He can completely save those who come to Him through Christ, and He wants to use us to bring people to Him! So take heart! Even when we cannot see the fruit of our labors, we can trust that God is using us to produce the eternal fruit of salvation in the lives of those we minister to. So, stay faithful and keep preaching.

As we remember that God can save completely, we can have confidence in our preaching and ministry. Even when we feel inadequate or unworthy, we can trust that God uses us for His purposes. We can rest in the promise that our preaching is not in vain.

So, as you labor in your ministry, remember that God wants to use you to produce the eternal fruit of salvation. Even in seasons of dryness or unfruitfulness, trust that God is at work and that your efforts are not in vain. May you find encouragement and strength in knowing God can completely save those who come to Him through Christ. And may God bless you and keep you, and may His love and grace sustain you always.

Questions for Reflection:

1. How can you see the hand of God at work in your salvation?

2. How have you seen God's hand at work in your own ministry?

3. How do you want to see God's hand in your ministry now?

DAY 16

Jesus helps us by offering a better covenant based on better promises.

"But now He has obtained a more excellent ministry, to the extent that He is also the mediator of a better covenant, which has been enacted on better promises."

(HEBREWS 8:6)

Pastor,

The ministry Jesus has called us is far better than we often realize. We diligently labor to do the ministry we are called to in many ways that people fail to see. This can be exhausting and compounded when we do not see immediate fruit.

This can tempt us to double down on our own efforts to see results. It can tempt us to trust our talents and abilities rather than the good news of the Gospel of Jesus that we proclaim week in and week out. It can be easy for us to fall into the trap of relying on our works to please God and bring about His kingdom. However, the book of Hebrews 8:6 reminds us of a much better way of trusting in ourselves–we trust in a better covenant based on better promises.

This verse reminds us that Jesus has received a superior ministry and established a better covenant than the one based on works and rules. The new covenant, the much better one, is based on grace and the promises of God. Pastors, as much as anyone, must remember that we are saved and made new through Jesus' sacrifice and the promises of God and not in what we do. Still, this

DAY 16

is also the basis for our ministry. It is not about our talent or efforts; it is about Him and His gracious work! So, trust in the better covenant than the one based on works and trust in His finished work, even in our own ministries! Trust in Him and not in our ministry.

Instead of laboring in your strength, know that Jesus has established a better covenant based on better promises. Trust that these promises extend not just to your faith but also to the work you do. Emphasize His grace and love in your ministry, and trust in Him to bring about His Kingdom in and through you and your service to Him.

Dear pastor, trust in this glorious covenant of grace, and may the Lord bless you and guide you in your ministry.

Questions for Reflection:

1. Why is it vital for you to remember the Gospel of grace in your own life?

2. What are you trying to do right now in your own strength?

3. How is it freeing to know that God actually wants to work through you?

DAY 17

Jesus helps us by reminding us of the power of His forgiveness.

"For I will be merciful toward their wrongdoings, And their sins I will no longer remember."

(HEBREWS 8:12)

Pastor,

    As the undershepherd of your church, you are constantly pouring out your heart and soul to minister to other peoples' needs. You offer encouragement, guidance, and support to those who come to you seeking hope and healing. But as much as you minister to others, it's important to remember that *you*, too, need to be reminded of the forgiveness found only in the work of Christ.

    If we are honest, we often feel that our sins are too great for God to use us in ministry, and we can allow these feelings to make us feel like failures. But Hebrews 8:12 is a powerful reminder that God's forgiveness is available to *all* who come to Him in faith, us included!

    We need to remember Christ's forgiveness as we labor for Him, knowing that it is only His forgiveness that justifies us and qualifies us to serve Him.

    Pastor, you need Christ's forgiveness every bit as much as the members of your church. So, don't let guilt or shame keep you from receiving Christ's love and mercy. Take time to confess your sins and allow His forgiveness to wash over you. Rest in His goodness and grace as you labor. Trust in His mercy and love as you encourage others to do the same. Remember that God has forgotten our sins through the precious blood of His Son, and, as a result, He looks at us as redeemed people and as redeemed pastors. Dwell, not on your past or struggles but in God's goodness.

Pastor, as you minister to others, may you be filled with this beautiful assurance of God's forgiveness, grace, and love, knowing that you have been set free in Christ to do the excellent work of the Gospel.

Questions for Reflection:

1. Why is it a good reminder that pastors need daily grace in our lives and ministry?

2. How can the busyness of the ministry keep us from remembering God's grace toward us?

3. When we do not dwell in the grace of God, how is our ministry crippled?

DAY 18

Jesus helps us by reminding us to persevere in faith, even when things are hard.

"And just as it is destined for people to die once, and after this *comes* judgment, so Christ also, having been offered once to bear the sins of many, will appear a second time for salvation without *reference to* sin, to those who eagerly await Him."

(HEBREWS 9:27–28)

Pastor,

There can be beautiful times of such great sweetness in ministry. Seeing people come to faith. Baptisms. Births. Seeing people surrender to God's call. Vacation Bible School. Gospel-centered funerals. So, many times, we get to see the rewarding fruit of our efforts for the Gospel.

However, there are times of sadness and grief in our ministry. Adultery. Divorce among families we serve. Sin that destroys. Gossip, slander, lies. Rejection. Deaths that grieve us to the core. The difficulties we all face in ministry are far too many to count. And they are far too painful to minimize. But Jesus is our great High Priest, and He truly knows what we are going through.

But there is excellent news for us to consider amid our pain: Jesus will return! This is a fact and a gracious truth that can allow our times of ministry difficulty to be reminders of grace. For fellow pastors, it is only by looking to the future–the final end of our

DAY 18

earthly work–that we can be reminded that God will reward those of us who labor and eagerly wait for Him.

As we labor *now*, we keep our eyes on the eventual return of Jesus that is to *come*. This reminds us to persevere through our hardships, knowing they will be rewarded by Jesus, who sees and knows all.

Jesus helps us by reminding us to persevere in faith, even when things are difficult, and we are overwhelmed, exhausted, or discouraged. Because, even during these difficulties, we find great hope in the promise of Christ's return. Because it is through the promise of His return that we know we have something to look forward to, even in the reality of our present struggles. So we eagerly await this coming day when Jesus will return to set all things right, to wipe away our tears, and to bring us into his glorious kingdom. This hope sustains us, even in the darkest of times.

So when you are weary or discouraged, remember that Jesus is with you; more than that, He has surely promised to return. Hold fast to this truth, and know that your labor in the Lord is not in vain! Press on. Serve. Minister. Know that one glorious day, it will have all been worth it, and may the hope of Christ's return strengthen and encourage you as you serve him faithfully.

Questions for Reflection:

1. What current situation you are dealing with needs to be looked at with eternity in mind?

2. How can trusting in the return of Jesus help you remain faithful today?

3. What do you need to trust Jesus to do in your life?

DAY 19

Jesus helps us by offering Himself as the sacrifice for our sins once and for all.

"But He, having offered one sacrifice for sins for all time, sat down at the right hand of God."

(HEBREWS 10:12)

Pastor,

Jesus' death on the cross for sin is the most extraordinary event in history. We know this. We preach this. We believe this. But how often are we genuinely encouraged by this? We remind people almost every week that their sins have been forgiven, but how often do we stop to consider the glorious truth that Jesus has died once for *our* sin?

When was the last time we dwelt on the goodness and grace of our loving Christ who sacrificed Himself for us, not because of who we were but because of who He is? Jesus helps us in ministry because He has freely offered Himself as the propitiation of our sins. And He has done this out of His obedience to His Father and His great love for us.

As we pastor our people, this is a freeing thought because it reminds us that we receive the same grace we preach. Fellow pastor, Jesus died for your church members' sins but also died to save you. Live in this wondrous truth of grace and mercy.

Remember that as followers of Jesus, we know that we have been forgiven of our sins. However, this forgiveness doesn't mean

DAY 19

we can continue to live in sin. We must daily choose to crucify our old sinful selves and walk in the newness of life that Christ has offered us. Let us remember the depth of Jesus' atoning sacrifice for us, but live our lives as a testimony to this infinite love and grace.

Die to self. Die to sin. Live to Christ. Live to grace. As we model this in our spiritual lives, we have a tangible example to those around us of God's grace to all people!

Pastor, remember to preach the Gospel of *good news* to yourself first. Remember that God's grace was showered upon you just as much as it should be on the people you serve.

Questions for Reflection:

1. Why is it sometimes hard for us to find solace in God's forgiveness to us?

2. What aspect of your life needs to be reminded of God's good grace to you?

3. How can resting in God's grace make you a better pastor?

DAY 20

Jesus helps us by giving us the strength to endure trials and persecution.

"But remember the former days, when, after being enlightened, you endured a great conflict of sufferings...Therefore, do not throw away your confidence, which has a great reward. For you have need of endurance, so that when you have done the will of God, you may receive what was promised."

(HEBREWS 10:32, 35–36)

Pastor,

As you run the race that God has called you, it can be tempting to tap out or quit as we encounter all the difficulties accompanying pastoral ministry. In light of these difficulties, becoming discouraged and losing sight of the goal can be easy. But look at the encouraging words in Hebrews 10:32–39.

These verses encourage us to endure the suffering in ministry. Just like athletes who train hard and persevere through the pain of training to reach their intended goal, we, too, must focus on Jesus Christ and endure the suffering that comes with the ministry that He has entrusted us with. When we focus on Jesus, we are reminded that He also suffered greatly for us. But it also reminds us that His suffering had a purpose. Jesus endured the cross because of the joy set before him (Hebrews 12:2). Still, He also endured this great suffering for the reward promised to Him..

DAY 20

In the same way, we, too, can endure suffering in ministry by focusing on the joy and reward that awaits us! We can endure the pain and hardship of ministry because we know we are doing the Lord's will. Still, we can also endure because we know a great and eternal reward awaits us in heaven.

So, my dear pastors, do not give up. Do not tap out. Do not lose heart, and do not lose sight of the goal. Keep your eyes fixed on Jesus and endure whatever suffering comes with your ministry. Remember that your suffering also has a purpose and that a great reward awaits you and others who will benefit from your faithfulness.

Run your race faithfully. Run it with endurance. Run it *knowing* that you will receive what is promised.

Questions for Reflection:

1. What is one area of your ministry you know you are not running with endurance?

2. What is one area of your life that you might need to give up to be more faithful in another?

3. How can you personally train more efficiently to be better equipped to run with endurance?

DAY 21

Jesus helps us by assuring us that we are saved through faith in Him.

"But we are not among those who shrink back to destruction, but of those who have faith for the safekeeping of the soul."

(HEBREWS 10:39)

Pastor,

    The most crucial aspect of your life is not that you are a pastor or minister of the Gospel. The talents and giftedness that God has equipped you with might be impressive to many, but, ultimately, they are not that big of a deal, nor do they even qualify you to do the work you are entrusted with.

    No. The most crucial aspect of your life is that you are forgiven of your sin and justified before a righteous and holy God. The assurance of your salvation is the most important aspect of your life. The fact that God would choose to use people like us is humbling and, rightly so. But the fact that Jesus would die on the cross for us, as sinful as we are, is the most humbling fact of all. We stand redeemed, not because of our service to Him but because of His great service to us!

    It is easy to get caught up in our accomplishments in the ministry, but let me remind you of this truth: neither our salvation nor our ministry is something we have earned or deserved, but is a free gift from God. This truth should humble us and keep us from having pride in who we are or what we do, but it should also remind us that everything good in our lives is simply because of God's good grace towards us. Our talents, abilities, achievements, and ministries are all gifts from God, and we should use them to bring glory to Him!

As pastors, we have been entrusted with a great responsibility to preach the Gospel and shepherd the flock. Still, we must remember that our strength or wisdom does not enable us to do this effectively. Still, it is only by God's good grace that we can fulfill this calling.

So, fellow pastor, let us humble ourselves and realize that we are saved by His work for us on the cross, and let us humbly embrace the calling He has entrusted us with to serve and glorify Him.

May we never forget that it is only because of God's good grace towards us that we have anything good in our lives, including our ministries.

Questions for Reflection:

1. What aspect of our ministries are you currently prideful about?

2. What is one area of your ministry that you need to repent of?

3. How can your pride hinder the work of God in your life and ministry?

DAY 22

Jesus helps us by reminding us of the faith and perseverance of those who have gone before us

"All these died in faith..."

(HEBREWS 11:13)

Pastor,

Hebrews 11 is a testimony of the faithful and a reminder that we all stand on the shoulders of those who have gone before us. When we encounter the challenges and difficulties often accompanying ministry, it may be easy to question whether it is worth it. But let me remind you of the *great cloud of witnesses* who have gone before us and their faith and perseverance that can inspire us to remain faithful in our present circumstances.

Hebrews 11 tells us about many faithful people who trusted God's promises and endured great trials and hardships. We read about Abel, Enoch, Noah, Abraham, Sarah, Isaac, Jacob, Joseph, Moses, Rahab, and many others who trusted in God and persevered through the difficulties that surrounded them. These men and women of faith did not have all the answers, and they did not always know what the future held. But, despite their challenges, they faithfully trusted in God's promises and were willing to follow Him wherever He led them. Their incredible examples encourage us to remain faithful in our present, even when it is difficult.

Like them, we may not always know what our future holds, but we can trust God's promises. We can trust in God's faithfulness.

We can trust in God's goodness. We can trust in God Himself. We, like them, can trust in God's plan and calling in our lives as we seek to be faithful to what He has called us.

As pastors, we have been called to serve God and shepherd His people, and this calling will come with its challenges and difficulties that make us feel ill-equipped. But let us remember the example of those who went before us, and let us be inspired by their faith and perseverance.

Pastor, let us fix our eyes on Jesus Christ, the author and perfecter of our faith, and let us trust in His glorious promises and His infinite faithfulness to see us through the challenges of ministry and may we be faithful and obedient to His call, knowing that He will never leave us nor forsake us!

Questions for Reflection:

1. Who are some people you are grateful to for the example they set in ministry?

2. How can you be an example to other ministers in fulfilling your calling?

3. How is it encouraging that a *great cloud of witnesses* have gone before you in ministry?

DAY 23

Jesus helps us by reminding us of the power of prayer.

"And without faith it is impossible to please *Him*, for the one who comes to God must believe that He exists, and *that* He proves to be One who rewards those who seek Him."

(HEBREWS 11:6)

Pastor,

How often do we attempt great things for God in our own strength? If we are honest, this is often the norm, isn't it? We know what God's word says, so we sometimes fail to immerse ourselves in it. We know–or think we know–what God wants from us, so we often lead without seeking Him. We tend to trust our instincts because we feel that we have the proper experience, and, after all, we are the pastor, so surely we know best. . .

But do we? Do we really know what is best? Or do we *assume* we know best? Hebrews 11:6 reminds us that Jesus will reward His followers only if we seek Him. This means that we must draw near to Him and seek Him through prayer.

Ministry is an important and noble task, but we must do it through God's strength and not our own abilities. Too often, we forget this. Or we simply assume that we are doing what we do with His blessing or approval. But how can we know if we do not truly seek Him through prayer?

Fellow pastors, we must repent of seeking to do God's ministry without truly seeking Him in the midst of it. Jesus modeled

DAY 23

this for us in His ministry, for He would often withdraw to lonely places to pray and seek His Father's will and guidance. If Jesus modeled this Himself, why do we often skip out on the process?

So let us also be people of faith who earnestly seek God in prayer and trust in the wisdom and guidance that only He can give. Let us not rely on our strength, abilities, and understanding but seek to please Him by seeking His will in everything we say or do.

May we seek His will and follow the path that He leads us by faithfully trusting in His good plan at every step. Only by doing this can we have genuine and lasting success in our labors. But, take heart: He promises to reward those who do!

Questions for Reflection:

1. Why is it so easy for us to trust in our own strengths?

2. What must you do to better seek the Lord in your ministry?

3. What is one area in your life and ministry that you fully need to surrender to the Lord through prayer?

DAY 24

Jesus helps us by reminding us of the ultimate reward that awaits us.

"All these died in faith, without receiving the promises, but having seen and welcomed them from a distance, and having confessed that they were strangers and exiles on the earth. For those who say such things make it clear that they are seeking a country of their own. And indeed if they had been thinking of that *country* which they left, they would have had opportunity to return. But as it is, they desire a better *country*, that is, a heavenly one. Therefore God is not ashamed to be called their God; for He has prepared a city for them."

(HEBREWS 11:13–16)

Pastor,

Do you love your church? Do you love the community where you minister? This is a great thing and a daily reminder of God's grace toward you. But, no matter how much you love your place of ministry, it is broken, flawed, and desperately in need of the Gospel. After all, this is one of the reasons that you are faithful to minister where you have been called.

As you continue to serve faithfully, you may encounter challenges and difficulties that can discourage you or even doubt your calling or effectiveness. But let us remember the words of Hebrews 11:13–16, which remind us of the ultimate reward that awaits us in eternity. Like those who have gone before us in faith, we, too, are

DAY 24

"strangers and exiles" here. We are not meant to find our ultimate satisfaction and reward in the things of this world–or even in our ministries. Instead, we are to seek a better *country* that awaits us in heaven.

When we face challenges and difficulties in ministry, it can be easy to lose sight of this ultimate reward and destination. We can become so focused on the here and now that we forget that this place is not our real home. But Jesus helps us by reminding us of the ultimate reward awaiting us.

Despite the flaws that this world may have, let us fix our eyes on Jesus, who endured the cross for the joy that was set before him. He knew that the ultimate reward was not found in this world, but in the presence of the Father in heaven. Remember that the coming kingdom is far better than the broken world we have been called to love. Let us remember that this world is not our home.

So, let us be encouraged by the words of Hebrews 11, and let us keep our eyes fixed on the *ultimate* reward that awaits us. May we be faithful in our present ministry, knowing that our labor is not in vain, but let us know and trust that we will one day receive the ultimate reward of being with our Savior forever!

Questions for Reflection:

1. What is it that you love most about your church and community?

2. How is it good to know that God will fully redeem these characteristics in heaven?

3. How can we sometimes love *here* more than we love *there*?

DAY 25

Jesus helps us by reminding us of the importance of living by faith, not by sight.

"By faith..."

(HEBREWS 11)

Pastor,

Everything that we do must be done "by faith." But this is the challenge, isn't it? In a day where we *see* so much, it is often difficult to seek to live by faith because we are practical people of modern means. It can be very easy to become prideful in our ministry by relying on our understanding. As a result, it can be easy to forget that everything we have is a gift from God, who loves us.

But as Hebrews 11 reminds us, we are called to live and do ministry by faith and not by our limited human sight. Chapter 11 begins with the definition of faith: "Now faith is the assurance of things hoped for, the conviction of things not seen." So, faith requires us to trust God even when we cannot see the results or the path ahead.

Throughout the chapter, we see examples of those who lived by faith, including Abel, Enoch, Noah, Abraham, Sarah, Isaac, Jacob, and Joseph. They all trusted God's promises and acted accordingly, even when they could not see the end result. As pastors, we, too, are called to live by faith, trusting in God's promises and guidance even when we cannot see the end result, which is quite often. There is far too much outside our control, so we must not rely on our own understanding but instead seek God's wisdom and guidance in all we do.

Let us be reminded that the source of our strength and success in ministry is not ourselves, our talent, or our abilities but God Himself. Let us boast not in our accomplishments, however good they may seem, but in the work God is doing through us as we do what He has called us.

We must live by faith and not by sight, so we must live and do ministry by faith, trusting in God's promises and guidance every step of the way. When we live by sight, we begin to trust in ourselves more often than we should, which almost always leads us to pride. This pride in ourselves and our work will lead us to trust ourselves rather than God. This is not the way to God-honoring ministry. It is the way of death because it is the way of pride.

Pastor, we cannot see. We are blind. We are broken. Trusting in what we see may occasionally lead to temporary success, but it will never lead to lasting faithfulness. Instead, our pride must be replaced with humility as we seek to honor God and serve his people with faith and obedience that can only come from faith in Him.

Questions for Reflection:

1. How are you wrongfully trusting your own sight in your ministry now?

2. What must you do to live by faith in what God has called you?

3. How do you need to see your faith stretched and grown in your current season of life and ministry?

DAY 26

Jesus helps us by being the author and perfecter of our faith

"Therefore, since we also have such a great cloud of witnesses surrounding us, let's rid ourselves of every obstacle and the sin which so easily entangles us, and let's run with endurance the race that is set before us, looking only at Jesus, the originator and perfecter of the faith, who for the joy set before Him endured the cross, despising the shame, and has sat down at the right hand of the throne of God."

(HEBREWS 12:1–2)

Pastor,

Our faith is not our own. It is a beautiful gift from a good, glorious, and gracious God. This is good news for the weary pastor. Since we labor so much in the ministry, we can often focus more on what *we* are doing rather than what *God* is doing.

Jesus is the author and perfecter of our faith, which also means He is the author and perfecter of our ministries. This is good news for the weary pastor because ministry can be a challenging and draining experience. But let us be encouraged by the truth that Jesus is the author and perfecter of our faith and also of our ministry. So, we must fix our eyes on Jesus.

But what does it mean for Jesus to be the author and perfecter of our ministry? It means that He is the one who has called us to ministry in the first place, but it also means that He is the one who

DAY 26

will sustain us and guide us through every challenge and obstacle that we face! Again, this is good news for us!

We are not called to rely on our strength, wisdom, talent, or ability; instead, we are to trust in the power and guidance of the Holy Spirit. As we surrender our ministry to Jesus, He *will* guide, empower, and bring fruit from our labor; more than that, He will *perfect* our labors.

Let us be encouraged by Philippians 1:6, which reminds us, "that he who began a good work in you will bring it to completion at the day of Jesus Christ." In other words, Jesus is the one who began the good work of ministry in us, and He is also the one who will carry it on to completion.

So let us fix our eyes on Jesus, the author and perfecter of our faith and ministry, and trust in His guidance and strength. Let us find rest in the knowledge that He is with us every step of our way, and may our weariness be replaced with joy as we faithfully serve the Lord!

Questions for Reflection:

1. How is it good news to know that Jesus is the author and perfecter of our faith and ministry?

2. Why is it so easy to give ourselves credit for what God is doing in our lives?

3. What do you need to repent to give God the honor He deserves?

DAY 27

Jesus helps us by being the source of our joy and strength in life.

"Therefore, since we also have such a great cloud of witnesses surrounding us, let's rid ourselves of every obstacle and the sin which so easily entangles us, and let's run with endurance the race that is set before us, looking only at Jesus, the originator and perfecter of the faith, who for the joy set before Him endured the cross, despising the shame, and has sat down at the right hand of the throne of God."

(HEBREWS 12:1-2)

Pastor,

As we go through the ups and downs of ministry, it can be easy to lose sight of our joy. But let me remind you that your joy is not found in what you do. It is not found in your ministry successes. It can not be lost because of your ministry failures. Your joy can only be found in Jesus.

Hebrews 12:1-2 reminds us that Jesus endured the cross because of the joy that accompanied fulfilling the will of His Father. We consider who He is and what He has done for us, leading us to a fountain of joy in our lives and ministries..

Jesus is the supreme source of all lasting joy. He did not find joy in the pain and suffering of the cross but in the knowledge that through His sacrifice, He would bring salvation to all who believe in Him. In the same way, our ministry may bring pain and suffering. Still, this pain and suffering lead to gospel-ministry fruit, which can bring joy as we see lives transformed by the Gospel. The fruit should help motivate and sustain us through our ministry.

When you feel weary and discouraged, remember that Jesus endured opposition from sinful men. Jesus endured pain and suffering. Jesus had to run the race set before Him, just as we do. He understands the difficulties of ministry and is with you every step of the way. Dear pastor, ignore the problems, fix your eyes on Him, and let His joy be your strength.

Don't let the demands of your ministry rob you of the inner joy found in Christ. Instead, let your ministry be a tangible overflow of the joy you have found in Him and run the race before you in faith. As you continue to serve Him faithfully, may you find renewed strength and joy in knowing that you are doing His will.

May God bless you and fill you with His joy, knowing that He who endured much for us will equip you to be faithful to Him. He is worthy, and He is worth it.

Stay the course and run your race.

Questions for Reflection:

1. What are you focusing on now that is keeping you from true and lasting joy?

2. What do you need to give up to experience joy?

3. What do you need to stop looking at or worry about to keep your eyes on Christ?

DAY 28

Jesus helps us by disciplining us for our good.

"For the moment, all discipline seems not to be pleasant, but painful; yet to those who have been trained by it, afterward it yields the peaceful fruit of righteousness."

(HEBREWS 12:11)

Pastor,

A good father disciplines his children, and so does our Heavenly Father discipline us, His beloved children. Just as a loving parent disciplines their child to correct behavior and teach valuable life lessons, so does our Heavenly Father discipline us to help mold us more into His Son's image and bring about our much-needed spiritual growth.

Pastors need spiritual discipline just as much as church members. So, you may face discipline from God as you seek to lead and guide your congregation. While it may not be pleasant in the present, we must rest assured that it will yield good fruit in our lives and ministries in due season.

Remember that discipline is not the same thing as punishment; instead, it is a loving act of correction meant for our good. Just as a child may not understand the reasoning behind their parent's discipline, we may not always understand why God allows certain things to happen in our lives. Therefore, do not lose heart when facing various trials and difficulties in your life or ministry. Instead, see them as a beautiful opportunity to grow in your faith and character, trusting that His discipline is for your good and will ultimately lead to greater spiritual maturity.

We must be reminded that discipling a child is a loving act for a parent. So, a disciplined child is significantly loved by their parents. Look at God's discipline similarly: it is rooted in love for us, His children, and is meant to make us stronger! As you face the trials and challenges of ministry, may you be encouraged by the knowledge that God loves you enough to discipline you. He loves your ministry enough to discipline you to make you more effective!

Trust in His loving plan and know He works all things together for your good, even through godly discipline.

Questions for Reflection:

1. What are some areas that you need to seek spiritual discipline?

2. What areas have you been looking at as punishment but, in actuality, have been loving discipline from a loving Father?

3. How might you use God's discipline toward you to encourage others to submit to God's discipline in their lives?

DAY 29

Jesus helps us by providing our peace and security.

Make sure that your character is free from the love of money, being content with what you have; for He Himself has said, "I will never desert you, nor will I ever abandon you," so that we confidently say,

"The Lord is my helper, I will not be afraid.
What will man do to me?"

(Hebrews 13:5–6)

Pastor,

You may serve a local church, but you must rest assured that you work for the Lord. The church treasurer may sign your check, but the Lord supplies your needs.

God's promise to never leave or forsake us reminds us that we can trust Him with every aspect of our lives, including our finances. As a pastor, it can be easy to fear what people in your church may think or do regarding financial matters. But remember that the Lord is your helper, and you can confidently trust Him.

Hebrews 13:5 reminds us to keep our lives free from the love of money. But that does not mean we should be unconcerned with money because it is also how we put groceries on our family's table. In this way, we are no different from our church members. However, keeping your life free from the *love* of money and being content is still crucial.

DAY 29

As you focus on the work of ministry, trust that God will provide for your needs. So, as we trust Him to provide, stay faithful to His calling on your life, and know He will take care of you. Do not allow earthly worry to keep you from leading well. Trust in His goodness and tender care, and trust that He will provide for you as you work for Him.

Think of it this way: just as a shepherd cares for his flock, the Lord cares for His children. Just as a shepherd provides for the needs of his sheep, so does the Lord provide for the needs of His children. Trust in Him and know He is faithful to keep His promises, for you are loved and cared for just like any other sheep.

As you navigate the financial aspects of your life, family, and ministry, may you be encouraged by the promise that the Lord is your helper and that He will never leave nor forsake you. Stay faithful to the calling He has placed on your life, and trust in Him to provide for your every need.

May God bless you and guide you as you continue to serve Him, trusting Him to be your provider and sustainer. Do not worry about finances.

Questions for Reflection:

1. What are some past ways that God has provided for your needs?

2. What is a financial need in your life that you need to trust God to provide?

3. Is there something you need to change in your life to be more financially responsible?

DAY 30

Jesus helps us by empowering us to offer sacrifices of praise and good deeds.

"Through Him then, let's continually offer up a sacrifice of praise to God, that is, the fruit of lips praising His name. And do not neglect doing good and sharing, for with such sacrifices God is pleased."
(HEBREWS 13:15–16)

Pastor,

How good it is to serve the Lord with our lives!

God could have called anyone to do His work, but He chose you! How incredible and humbling this is! He has called us to serve Him through our ministry, and this ought to be a source of our praise as we seek to do good deeds for Him.

Hebrews 13:15–16 reminds us that, as pastors, we are called to do good works through ministry. Still, we must also remember to continually offer up a sacrifice of praise to God while we do them. Amid the challenges and difficulties that come with ministry, it can be easy to lose sight of the goodness of God. It can be easy to do our ministry out of duty or obligation rather than delight and joy. However, even in difficult seasons of ministry, it's important to remember that God is good and that all good things come from Him. As we seek to do good deeds for Him through our ministry, remember to praise Him for His goodness and grace.

Offering up a sacrifice of praise can be challenging. It may require us to push through our discouragement, frustration, and doubt, but it is always worth it because God is always good to us! Praising God during our ministry is a powerful reminder that we are not alone in our work. God is with us, working through us to accomplish His will.

Think of it this way: as we seek to do good works, we shine like a candle in the darkness. And as we offer up our sacrifice of praise, we are like a beacon of light, shining brightly for all to see. Let us never forget the importance of praising God in our ministry, even when it may be difficult.

So as you go about your ministry, remember to praise God for His goodness and offer a sacrifice of praise, acknowledging His name and giving Him the glory that He rightly deserves. And as you do good works and share with others, know that these sacrifices are pleasing to God and be reminded that the ministry that He has called you to is an honor and a blessing.

May God bless you and guide you as you continue faithfully serving Him. Remember, He is worthy of all our praise.

Questions for Reflection:

1. What are you excited about in your ministry right now?

2. How can you be more grateful for all God has called you to do?

3. What can you do differently to be more productive in ministry?

www.ingramcontent.com/pod-product-compliance
Lightning Source LLC
Chambersburg PA
CBHW071753040426
42446CB00012B/2534